FRIENDS *forever!*

Paintings by SUSAN WINGET

HARVEST HOUSE PUBLISHERS

EUGENE, OREGON

Wear somethin that makes you smile today!

FRIENDS FOREVER!

A perfect match

Put your best
foot
forward !

The language of friendship is not words but meanings.

HENRY DAVID THOREAU

Attention to detail is the secret of success in

every sphere of life. Little kindnesses, little acts

of consideration, little appreciations, and little

confidences are all that most of us are called

on to perform, but they are all that are

needed to keep a friendship sweet.

HUGH BLACK
Friendship

Laugh Love Shop

We've shared so much *laughter,* so many *tears.*

We're a spiritual bond that *grows stronger* each year.

We're not *sisters* by birth, but we knew from the start,

Something put us together to be *sisters of the heart.*

AUTHOR UNKNOWN

WHAT A LUXURY IT WAS TO SPEND TIME
WITH OLD FRIENDS WITH WHOM IT WAS OKAY
TO TALK ABOUT NOTHING MUCH.

LISA ALTHER

It seems to me that trying to live

without friends is like milking a bear

to get cream for your morning coffee.

It is a whole lot of trouble, and not

worth much after you get it.

ZORA NEALE HURSTON

It doesn't matter what we do...
I always love my time with you

My best friend is the one who brings out the best in me.

I had rather have a robin

for a friend than a swallow; for a swallow

abides with us only in the summer time,

but a robin cometh to us in the winter.

CHARLES SPURGEON

Constant use will not wear ragged the fabric of friendship.

DOROTHY PARKER

Let us be grateful to people
who make us happy;
they are the charming gardeners who make our souls blossom.

MARCEL PROUST

The mind never unbends itself so agreeably
as in the conversation of a well-chosen friend. There is
indeed no blessing of life that is any way comparable to
the enjoyment of a discreet and virtuous friend. It eases and
unloads the mind, clears and improves the understanding,
engenders thought and knowledge, animates virtue and
good resolutions, soothes and allays the passions, and finds
employment for most of the vacant hours of life.

JOSEPH ADDISON

Just thinking about a friend

makes us want to do a *happy dance,*

because a *friend* is someone

who *loves you* in spite of your faults.

CHARLES SCHULZ

Good Friend

Listen

Soul friendships
are the safety net
of the heart.

SUSAN JEFFERS

*Friendship is the golden thread
that ties the heart of all the world.*

JOHN EVELYNN

My friends have made the story of my life.
In a thousand ways they have turned my limitations
into beautiful privileges, and enabled me to walk
serene and happy in the shadow cast
by my deprivation.

HELEN KELLER

IT TAKES A LONG TIME
TO GROW AN OLD FRIEND.

JOHN LEONARD

A FRIEND LOVES AT ALL TIMES.

THE BOOK OF PROVERBS

A true friend is the gift of God, and he only who made hearts can unite them.

ROBERT SOUTH

Some friendships are as comforting and
comfortable as a well-worn pair of shoes.
Others are full of excitement and adventure.
The best ones are laced with laughter
and softened with tears and strengthened
with a spiritual bond.

EMILIE BARNES AND DONNA OTTO
Friends of the Heart

*We are each other's reference point
at our turning points.*

ELIZABETH FISHEL

Friendship is the strangest but greatest thing in the world. I find my time with my friends the best times of my life. My friends are my heart, my soul, my fun, my laughter, tears, love, and my life.

KATE TIERNEY

I FEEL I AM MORE BLESSED THAN MANY PEOPLE
BECAUSE I HAVE THIS KIND OF A FRIEND IN MY LIFE.
A FRIEND WHO IS ALWAYS THERE FOR ME NO MATTER WHAT.
A FRIEND WHO ACCEPTS ME AS I AM BUT LOVES ME TOO MUCH
TO LET ME STAY THAT WAY. YES, I WOULD SAY I AM BLESSED
BECAUSE I HAVE A TRUE FRIEND.

ROBIN JONES GUNN
True Friends

There is nothing better than the
encouragement of a good friend.

KATHARINE BUTLER HATHAWAY

WHAT BRINGS JOY TO THE
HEART IS NOT SO MUCH
THE FRIEND'S GIFT AS THE
FRIEND'S LOVE.

ALFRED OF RIEVAULX

Once in a while you
meet someone
and soon you discover
the two of you are
truly something special
to each other...
you *share* your thoughts and feelings
so *relaxed* so openly,
and right away you knew
your friendship's *meant to be.*

GARY HARRINGTON

Friends are priceless

One can never have too many shoes!

Friendship is warmth in cold, firm ground in a bog.

MILES FRANKLIN

Friendship is the source of the greatest *pleasures,* and *without friends* even the most agreeable pursuits become *tedious.*

ST. THOMAS AQUINAS

The pleasure of your company is a many-sided affair. It includes
the pleasure of seeing you, the pleasure of hearing you talk,
the drama of watching your actions, your likes and dislikes and
adventures; the pleasure of hunting you up in your haunts,
and the delicate flattery we feel when you hunt us up in ours.

AUTHOR UNKNOWN

Life is a ship we sail... Girlfriends

re the anchor!

Yes, we must ever be friends;
and of all who offer you friendship
let me be ever the first, the truest,
the nearest and dearest!

HENRY WADSWORTH LONGFELLOW

I OFTEN THINK, HOW COULD I HAVE SURVIVED WITHOUT THESE WOMEN?

CLAUDETTE RENNER

Thus nature has no love for

solitude, and always leans, as it

were, on some support; and the

sweetest support is found in the

most intimate friendship.

CICERO

THE SHORTEST DISTANCE BETWEEN NEW FRIENDS IS A SMILE.

AUTHOR UNKNOWN

The friend in my adversity I shall always
cherish most. I can better trust those who
helped to relieve the gloom of my dark
hours than those who are so ready to enjoy
with me the sunshine of my prosperity.

ULYSSES S. GRANT

*A friend is someone who understands your past,
believes in your future, and accepts you today just*

ROBERT LOUIS STEVENSON

he way you are.

Friends...
Share Stories
Tell Jokes

Really Talk
Really Listen

In a friend you find a second self.

ISABELLE NORTON

Nothing opens the heart like a true friend.
to whom you may impart griefs. joys.
fears. hopes . . .
and whatever lies upon the heart.

FRANCIS BACON

Friendship is about *reciprocal* cherishing.

It may come as a *surprise* that to be a good friend

you might need to be able to *receive* loving care

as well as *give* it. But this is the essence of friendship.

ELISABETH YOUNG-BRUEHL AND FAITH BETHELARD

FRIENDSHIP IS THE ONLY CEMENT
THAT WILL EVER HOLD THE WORLD TOGETHER.

WOODROW WILSON

A FRIEND IS SOMEONE
WHO REACHES OUT
FOR YOUR HAND . . .
AND TOUCHES
YOUR HEART.

KATHLEEN GROVE

for girlfriends

I don't remember how
we happened to meet each other.
I don't remember who
got along with whom first.
All I can remember is all of us
together . . . always.

AUTHOR UNKNOWN

Friends warm you with their presence,
Trust you with their secrets,
And remember you in their prayers.

AUTHOR UNKNOWN

I HAVE LEARNED THAT TO BE WITH
THOSE I LIKE IS ENOUGH.

WALT WHITMAN